CONTEMPORARY MUSICIANS
AND THEIR MUSIC™

Avril Lavigne

Sarah Sawyer

ROSEN
PUBLISHING®
New York

To Karin Jacobson

Published in 2009 by The Rosen Publishing Group, Inc.
29 East 21st Street, New York, NY 10010

Copyright © 2009 by The Rosen Publishing Group, Inc.

First Edition

Library of Congress Cataloging-in-Publication Data

Sawyer, Sarah.
Avril Lavigne / Sarah Sawyer.—1st ed.
    p. cm.—(Contemporary musicians and their music)
Includes bibliographical references and index.
ISBN-13: 978-1-4042-1820-8 (library binding)
ISBN-13: 978-1-4358-5128-3 (pbk)
ISBN-13: 978-1-4042-7873-8 (6 pack)
1. Lavigne, Avril—Juvenile literature. 2. Singers—Canada—Biography—Juvenile literature. I. Title.
ML3930.L25S38 2008
782.42166092—dc22
[B]
                                                                    2008003923

Manufactured in Malaysia

On the cover: Avril Lavigne sings during a live performance.

Contents

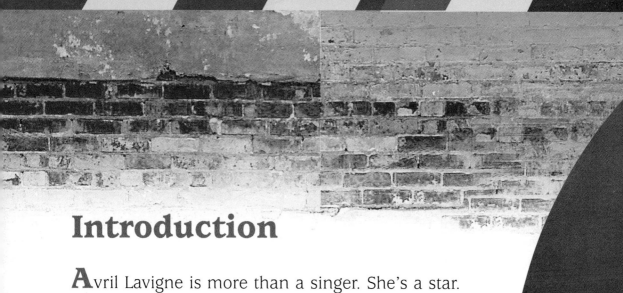

Introduction

Avril Lavigne is more than a singer. She's a star. Her mom knew it when she was a baby, and her fans know it today. Even *Rolling Stone*, the magazine often considered to be the first and last word on music culture, sees her as a standout from the crowd of current teen stars.

The 2004 *Rolling Stone Album Guide* describes her as a "pint-size 16-year-old hellion from the tiny Canadian town of Napanee, Ontario, with her kohl-rimmed eyes, baggy skateboarder's pants, a permanent scowl, [and a] whiff of punk to distinguish her from the Britneys and Christinas."

Avril Lavigne sings at the Zenith in Paris, France.

That's not all that sets her apart. She asserts her own personality and values in many ways. For instance, she's made a name for herself by refusing to do what lots of people think you need to do to be a pop star: showing her body off to gain fans and get attention. It's a choice she made purposefully, and she's very proud of it.

Why would she? She's certainly proven that she doesn't need to resort to such tactics. Her catchy tunes, confessional lyrics, and great attitude sell her records for her—lots of them! She's sold more than thirty-five million albums so far, which is a lot of CDs. Her first album, *Let Go* (2002), sold sixteen million copies and was certified six times platinum in the United States. Her next two releases, *Under My Skin* (2004) and *The Best Damn Thing* (2007), reached number 1 on the Billboard 200 listing. Under her pink-studded belt, she's got six number-1 songs and a grand total of eleven top-10 hits, including "Complicated," "Sk8er Boi," "I'm with You," "My Happy Ending," and "Girlfriend."

Chapter One

Avril's Early Life

When I was two my mom said she knew I was going to be a singer. I've been performing ever since I was a young kid. So I've known I wanted to do this for a while. I always knew in my heart that I'd be singing."

—*Avril Lavigne, imdb.com*

Avril Ramona Lavigne was born on September 27, 1984, to French-Canadian parents, Judy and John Lavigne. She is a middle child with an older brother, Matt, and a younger sister, Michelle. They all spent their early years as a family together in Napanee, Ontario, Canada.

Napanee was a great place for her to get her start. Situated on the water, with good schools and a healthy economy, it was an

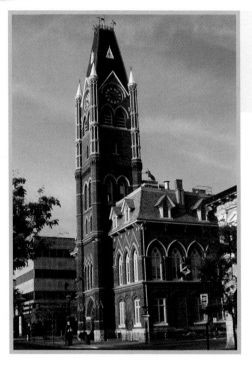

Belleville City Hall is one of the most charming landmarks found in Belleville, Ontario, where Lavigne was born.

ideal environment for raising children. Some Canadian cities have extraordinarily cold winters and no spring and fall to speak of—but not Napanee. The usual climate there is cold in the winter and hot in the summer, though not as warm as the Los Angeles Avril Lavigne came to know as she grew up.

Her very early years were not so different from other Canadian children. She was musical, but she was hardly a punkette baby. Almost the only thing we know about her very early life in music is that she sang country music, performed in her church choir, and taught herself to play guitar. "I started [singing] in church," she told Chad Dougatz for Yahoo! Music. "I went from gospel to country. When I started singing secular songs, it was country

Lavigne poses with her mother, Judy, at the release party for her album *The Best Damn Thing* in 2007.

music—just new country, not the whole twangy stuff. I sang a lot of Faith Hill, and Shania Twain, and Dixie Chicks."

Whoa! A little different from the Avril we know today, right? Would it surprise you to know that artists of many musical genres start with country music and church choirs? There's no written rule about this, of course, but it seems to happen over and over again. This might be because country music uses catchy, easier-to-sing melodies; is gentler on the vocal chords; and tends to have less adult language and topics. Country has always gravitated toward "family entertainment" more than rock and roll and punk. As country becomes more and more main-stream, this becomes less and less true, but many parents still seem to find country music the most acceptable for their kids.

Lavigne *(center)* stands with her brother, Matt, and sister, Michelle, backstage at the MuchMusic Awards in Toronto, Canada.

As for church choirs, many, many singers got their starts there. Everyone from Aretha Franklin (a.k.a. the Queen of Soul) to our own Avril Lavigne started their public singing careers by singing in their family's church choir. There are natural reasons for this, too. A church choir is generally a safe place for a young singer to develop his or her voice, learn more about music, and get used to singing in front of crowds. It's a place where parents are as welcome as kids; where the music isn't harmful to the vocal chords (like punk and rock can be because of the screaming); where the lyrics are clean and generally accepted for young people; and where the audience of family, friends, and acquaintances is likely to be supportive.

Lavigne started teaching herself to play guitar when she was about twelve. That's not unusual. Many musical people start with this fairly accessible instrument, probably because you don't really need any musical training or special education to get started. Chart books and Web sites make it easy to see which fingers go on which strings in order to form chords and other patterns. No matter how you learn, or which instrument you start with, playing an instrument is a lifelong pleasure and a great way for a young person to start paving his or her way in the world of music.

So, you're probably getting the picture that Avril Lavigne's early performances looked very different from the ones she gives now. She didn't go to church choir in leather and heavy eyeliner; she went dressed like other kids her age. And she performed at the same kinds of events that give many musicians their start: Sunday worship services, school musicals, chorale concerts, and Christmas pageants.

Avril Is Discovered

Of course, at some point Lavigne's lifestyle became very different from most teens. Music and practice became a big part of her life. "I worked really hard. I was really dedicated to my music," she told Chad Dougatz for Yahoo! Music. "My parents pushed me a lot. I would come home from school and I wouldn't be allowed to talk on the phone unless I'd spent a long time rehearsing, going over my songs."

It's a good thing she'd put so much time and energy into practice because something was about to happen that would get her on track to becoming a multiplatinum singer.

It was 1998 and, like any young singer hoping to become a rock star, Lavigne began singing in competitions and auditions. One of those competitions was for the chance to sing on stage with the famous Canadian country singer Shania Twain as she opened her first concert tour.

Lavigne showed up at a Chapters bookstore in Kingston, Ontario. (American readers can imagine this as a Barnes and Noble bookstore—they're similar in many ways.) She looked very

Shania Twain was one of Lavigne's early inspirations. She initially found much to emulate in Twain's energetic performances and clean country style.

different from the way you see her today. For starters, she was younger. She was also not wearing the pretty-in-punk fashions you're used to seeing her wear. She had a more clean-cut, preteen look at the time. And she was singing country, not rock and roll.

Even though the performance she gave was different from those that eventually made her a star, her star quality shone through. She won the competition, was given the opportunity to perform alongside Twain at her Ottawa concert, and was "discovered" by her first professional manager, Cliff Fabri.

Searching for a Record Contract

Having a manager meant Lavigne was in the musical big leagues. She now had someone looking out for her career in the way that only a professional manager can. Her manager helped her handpick the performances that would do the most to make her a star, and he helped her stay away from those that weren't quite right for her particular professional goals.

Lavigne was performing more and more and being seen by people who could help her make her dreams come true. A performance at the Lennox Community Theatre led to her being seen by Steve Medd, a popular local folk singer and relative of the well-connected and influential journalist Ben Medd. Steve invited her to sing on his song "Touch the Sky" for his 1999 album, *Quinte Spirit*, and then later on two tracks, "Temple of Life" and "Two Rivers," for his follow-up album, *My Window to You*. These were some of her first studio experiences; and while they were in a very different style from the one we know her for today, they helped her gain the experience and connections she would need as her career grew to superstar proportions.

This is how things went for a while. One connection at a time, she proved her talent and professionalism to people who could give her bigger gigs and better connections. Then finally, at the still very young age of sixteen, she got her biggest break yet. She got a record deal.

Every upstart band or soloist dreams of getting their first record deal. That first deal is the gateway to a whole new professional life. It is the first step toward being a star. For Lavigne, this break came in the person of Ken Krongard, who was the artists and repertoire (A&R) representative of Arista Records. He saw her talent, knew she could be a hit with young audiences, and wanted to do something to make that happen.

So, Lavigne moved to New York City to work on her debut album. Soon Krongard invited Antonio "L. A." Reid, the head of Arista Records, to stop by the studio and hear her sing. This was a big moment for her. There were powerful people gathered in the room, all intent on one question: Does Avril Lavigne have what it takes to be a sensational pop star?

The answer, of course, was a resounding YES!

What If . . .

Getting a manager changed things for Lavigne. When most kids and teens have a decision to make, they talk things over with their friends, their parents, and maybe someone from a church or school. Sound familiar? Is that how you make your decisions? Now, imagine that a manager was added to the crowd of people who help you make decisions. Imagine your parents talking to a manager to get advice about what's best for you. Imagine what might happen if your manager—the person who was helping you shape your future—had a disagreement with your parents, the people who loved you and raised you. That could get confusing very quickly, couldn't it?

Most of us want to make everyone happy, or at least as many people happy as possible. We want the adults around us to feel good about our decisions. But when there are big things happening—when it looks like you have a chance at stardom— sometimes you have to decide whether to take some risks.

Sometimes your adults support you in taking that risk; sometimes they don't. It's easy to imagine that those decisions aren't made without lots of talks, family meetings, and maybe a few emotional arguments.

It must have been a little like that when Lavigne, her manager, and her parents decided that she would drop out of high school and go to New York to work on her first album.

Of course, we all know that this decision was one of the many that made it possible for her to become a rock star. We know that because we see her in magazines, on the Internet, on television, in movies—almost everywhere we look.

What we don't see are the people who take the same gamble and lose. We don't hear about those teens because they don't become big stars. We don't see them in the media, in movies, and plastered in magazines and posters everywhere we look.

Imagine what the results of dropping out of school for a project that doesn't work out might be. If you're not sure, ask a school counselor or a teacher you trust to talk to you about it. Maybe, in Lavigne's case, she'd have just gone back to school and graduated a year later. Maybe she'd have taken her GED and missed senior year and graduation. Take a moment to think about the risk she took—and imagine what her life might be like

Lavigne sports her signature necktie as she celebrates the platinum status of her album *Let Go*.

if things had worked out differently. Is that a risk you'd feel OK taking? Do you think your parents would let you? Ask them sometime. You might be surprised by their answer.

What won't surprise you is learning that Avril Lavigne is 100 percent content with the decision she made and the risk she took. Because, of course, everything you've read so far led up to her releasing her first album and achieving amazing stardom. Keep reading—we're about to learn more about how she did it. Not only that, but we'll get into the really exciting part of this story: the music!

Chapter Two

The Music
of Avril Lavigne

As much as we might love her persona, her playfulness, and her way with fashion, it's the music that really draws fans to Avril Lavigne. In this chapter, we'll look at her current body of work and talk about some of the things that make her music so special.

About Critics

Critics sometimes get a bad reputation because they nitpick music. But they have to! It's their job. They take songs and think about every possible thing they can say about them—some good, some downright mean. You can decide for yourself how much you care what the critics have to say. After all, they're just people with opinions, just like you are. On the other hand, what they have that you might not have is a lot of practice describing music in such a way that even people who haven't heard it yet can imagine what it sounds like. For our purposes, we're going to examine some of the things that critics "in the know" most often say about Lavigne and try to form a picture of what makes her music work.

Avril Lavigne's Voice

It might seem obvious to you that a singing star should have a great voice—but that isn't always the case. Some singers are popular less for their voices than for their songwriting, their looks, their character, or some other trait they possess. While Avril

Lavigne has great looks, a fun character, and some songwriting skills, many critics agree that her appeal starts with her great voice!

Lavigne's engaging performance style includes dancing and crowd interaction—but never at the expense of her vocals. Here, she sings at the Jingle Ball in Madison Square Garden in 2007.

Reviewing *Let Go* for *Rolling Stone*, Pat Blashill wrote that nothing else "would matter if Lavigne didn't have a voice, equal parts baby girl and husky siren, that seems capable of setting off car alarms several city blocks away. As Lavigne wails over crashing waves of acoustic and electric guitars, her big voice occasionally turns sideways in a drawl, a casual hint that she may actually be, of all things, a fine country singer in the making. Truth be told, Lavigne has a great voice, a good shtick and a qualified staff of hitmakers."

While acknowledging her natural talent, Blashill also gave credit to the guidance of music industry pros for her winning voice. And isn't it interesting that he hears a slight "drawl" that makes him think of country music? It would be easy to think that all that time singing gospel and country was wasted once Lavigne found herself in punk, but maybe the strong singing and expressive lines that she learned from singing country music make her rock that much harder!

Her Songwriting

You might be thinking something like, "All of Avril's songs are so unique. How can we possibly talk about all of them at the same time?" Well, all of your friends look different, don't they? I bet you hardly ever get them confused. But that's because they look different on the surface. If we were to talk about their skeletons, they'd look much more similar, wouldn't they? They share bone structure—and so do most of Avril's Lavigne's songs.

Her songs—and most of the songs you hear on the radio—follow a very familiar verse-chorus song structure. Verses and choruses are the bones of a song. They're what make songs easy to sing and easy to remember. Most music listeners like to have a little bit of familiarity in their music. They like to know that parts of the song will repeat. That makes it easier to sing along, so most singer/songwriters, including Avril Lavigne, make good use of this structure.

There is usually an instrumental (no vocals) introduction, then verses followed by repetitions of a chorus. Simple, right? Now and then a bridge is thrown in for some variety. Most American pop songs written since the 1960s follow this form. Take, for example, the song "Contagious." It begins with a verse about some guy that the singer really likes. Then it goes into the chorus, which revolves around the rhyme of "contagious" and "outrageous." From there it goes into a second verse, a repetition of the chorus, and a bridge section. It ends by repeating the chorus twice.

Now that you've walked through this basic song structure once, you'll probably notice it, or a very similar structure, being repeated in many of your favorite pop songs. It's not song form that makes Lavigne's music so irresistible—it's the style layered on top of it!

Avril Lavigne's Musical Style

Two descriptors are most often used for Lavigne's music: punk and pop. She is a pop musician in that she uses the usual song form, performs in popular venues, and is played on top-40 radio and music-video channels. You may hear people refer to her music as bubblegum pop. This is a term that refers to highly processed pop music that's generally loved by younger audiences. It usually features catchy melodies, repeated riffs or musical hooks, an infectious rhythm, and a fairly simple song structure. Lyrically, bubblegum pop tends also to be on the lighter side. You will not have to wrack your brain to understand the meaning of a bubblegum pop tune.

This description no doubt fits Hilary Duff and *High School Musical*, for example, better than Avril Lavigne, but it is the base upon which Lavigne builds her style. Think of that description of bubblegum pop again while listening to "Complicated" or "Girlfriend." Can you hear things mentioned in that definition?

Rolling Stone thinks so. In its online bio of her, the magazine calls her songs "perfect pieces of sour-apple bubblegum music." What do you think is meant by that? Read on in the article and you'll find that it's saying Avril Lavigne's music is bubblegum pop spiked with a flaming shot of punk rock.

Punk is more than just loud guitars and heavy rhythms. It's an anti-establishment attitude. It's a way of not fitting the mold. It's a way of rebelling. In the 1970s and 1980s, punk bands such as the Sex Pistols, the Ramones, the Clash, and others defined the punk sound—and the punk look. There's something gritty, street level, and rough and tumble about punk. Lavigne fits that bill in some ways, but in others she's very different. She isn't grungy

High School Musical is one of the bigger acts in the genre of bubblegum pop.

or into drugs. Rather than the Sex Pistols' signature safety-pin piercing, Lavigne sports a single pink highlight in her freshly shampooed long, blonde hair. But she does use some punk-style chords and drum patterns, and she certainly would call herself anti-establishment.

Interview magazine has specialized in alternative culture for many, many years. One of its writers, Dimitri Ehrlich, can't decide if Avril Lavigne is more bubblegum than punk, or more punk than bubblegum. He's not alone. This question shows up in her reviews quite often. He did a particularly good job of tackling the question when he wrote: "As for the debate over her punk rock credentials, Lavigne is apathetic about punk despite being publicly associated with it. When she smashes her guitar in her videos it's as transgressive as someone blowing an air kiss. She sings

Singer Johnny Rotten performs with the Sex Pistols at their last concert together in 1978.

with a look of studied boredom that says, 'Whatever. Can I get back to shooting ducks?' [Growing up in Canada, Lavigne was known to do some bird hunting.] When you think about it, punk rock always was about flipping the bird to the world. And here she is, literally flipping birds out of the sky, making hits as if they were an afterthought, and yawning her way to the bank. What's more punk than that?"

From what Ehrlich wrote, we see that he grudgingly included Lavigne in the ranks of punk musicians. He's decided that her attitude, bubblegum or not, has enough punk in it to fit in with punk rock as he understands it.

There are lots of things about Avril Lavigne that are—pardon the pun—complicated. There's conflict in her style and aesthetic. But that's not the only place there is conflict. When it comes to Lavigne, there's one point that's debated more than all the others . . .

Does Avril Lavigne Write Her Own Songs?

It comes up again and again—and it's a hard issue to settle. Avril Lavigne and her management say one thing, and her collaborators say something else. Are they lying? Is she? Are they both telling a version of the truth? Probably.

There's nothing wrong with working with another songwriter, especially one who's more experienced. You can compare it to working with someone who is more skilled than yourself to make sure your English paper is as good as it can be. There's nothing wrong with asking for help.

What gets tricky in songwriting—as in doing homework—is the difference between asking for help and having someone else do your work for you. The songwriting team known as the Matrix, which worked with Lavigne on *Let Go*, claims that is what they did for her. They say that they did most of the songwriting and she takes credit for it as her own.

The *Canadian Press* reported, "One-time songwriting partner Lauren Christy, part of the hitmaking production team The Matrix ("Sk8er Boi" and "I'm With You"), suggested in a *Rolling Stone* article that the singer did little but 'change a word here or there.'"

Lavigne's side of the story: "I wanted to cry," she told *Entertainment Weekly* in a recent interview. "When you create something, and someone takes that away from you, it's like [they're taking away] your baby. Lauren and I would sing melodies and write lyrics together in the backyard on the blanket under an orange tree, and we had a great time. It was like a family. But . . .

Scott Spock, Lauren Christy, and Graham Edwards (members of the Matrix production team) attend the BMI Pop Awards in 2004.

they said some things and burned a bridge. I'm the biggest thing that ever happened to them."

So, for now, we don't know how much writing she does and how much is done for her. To date, when legal proceedings have been brought against Lavigne, her management has settled out of court, saying it's too expensive to try the case in court. Because there's been no trial, we don't know how much merit these claims have. Either way, there seems to have been hurt feelings and confusion on both sides, and a new determination on the part of Avril Lavigne to make it crystal clear that she does her own work.

"I told my manager: I'm doing this on my own!" Lavigne told *Entertainment Weekly*, speaking of her work on her third album, *The Best Damn Thing*. She claimed that her manager, BMG exec Clive Davis, agreed to let her work on her own, but she added, "I remember the label trying to be sneaky. They wanted to put this guy on my project. They were like, 'At least meet him,' and

WHO HELPS AVRIL LAVIGNE?

The Matrix, the production/writing team of Lauren Christy, Graham Edwards, and Scott Spock, cowrote many of Avril's Lavigne's songs. They are one of the hottest teams in American pop. They have cowriter and coproducer credits on Lavigne's album *Let Go*. The album was a big break for them, getting them a lot of attention and work from other singers. BMG Songs' president Scott Francis said in *Chart Attack* magazine, "The team's main strength is their ability to capture the essence of any artist, from Avril Lavigne to Ricky Martin to Liz Phair, and to deliver music with broad appeal."

I said no. I don't need anyone's opinion, advice, or help. I have my own vision, and they're my songs."

She's not a teenager anymore, and she's taking control of her career and her life!

Chapter Three

Avril, All Grown Up

When I first came out on the scene, I acted like a kid and dressed like a kid—and now I'm a woman. As you get older, you start dressing differently and doing things differently.

—*Avril Lavigne,* the Showbuzz

Avril Lavigne isn't seventeen anymore. She has changed both physically and mentally since she first took the stage as a gangly teenager. As a woman in her twenties, she's building an adult life for herself—and for her art. She got married and bought a house, and she is trying new things artistically. These are exciting rites of passage for her personally and fun things for her fans to see.

Avril Lavigne and Deryck Whibley's wedding made headlines in 2006. Here, they are at Antonio "L. A." Reid's fiftieth birthday party.

Her Marriage

On July 15, 2006, Avril Lavigne married Deryck Whibley, the front man of the Canadian rock band Sum 41. She was twenty-one and he was twenty-six. *People* magazine reported that her father walked her down the aisle to the sounds of the traditional wedding march. She wore a Vera Wang dress and carried white roses. They said their vows under a canopy of white flowers and had a beautiful reception after. Their first dance was to "Iris" by the Goo Goo Dolls.

Lavigne described her wedding to *Entertainment Tonight Canada*, saying, "It was perfect and beautiful. I'm used to going on stage and stuff but this was totally different. It was more exciting. It was the biggest moment of my life. I almost started crying as soon as I started walking down the first set of stairs. And I just told myself: 'You can't cry now, it's the beginning.' So I had to hold it

Lavigne shows her wedding ring to friends during her 2007 appearance on MTV's *TRL*.

all in and I wanted to keep my composure. And I did."

Sounds fairy-tale perfect, doesn't it? Well, before you imagine this happily married, young star singer and her rock star husband disappearing into their $9.5 million, three-story, Tuscan-style house complete with eight bedrooms, ten bathrooms, an elevator, an office, a steam shower, a sauna, a pool, and a ten-car garage, think again! Avril Lavigne's not ready to kick back and live happily ever after. She's still working hard and reaching for the stars!

Avril Lavigne's Acting Career

Lavigne's film credits to date include *Over the Hedge* with Bruce Willis, *Fast Food Nation* with Patricia Arquette, and *The Flock* with Richard Gere. She's had no starring dramatic roles yet but is quite content with her crossover achievements.

"I've had a singing career for five years. I'm ready to try out new stuff and have some fun," she said in an interview with Britain's *TV Hits* magazine. When asked what kind of acting she'd like to try, she replied, "I like more serious roles. I can see myself in something like *Girl Interrupted*. I would enjoy doing a film on the darker side, something serious with depth. I'm good at expressing myself and getting all my emotions out."

One role she was pleased with was that of the voice of the teenage possum, Heather, in the animated movie *Over the Hedge*. "I want to start off small and warm up," she told Derek Robins for Britain's *Sun*. "I wouldn't want to just throw myself into a big part. *Over the Hedge* was a great first film."

It's not surprising that she started with a role like Heather.

Lavigne poses with "Heather," the cartoon possum that she provided the voice for in the 2006 film *Over the Hedge*.

When artists cross from one medium, like music, to another—in this case, movies—there's often a short period where they play roles that are very much in keeping with the persona they enjoyed in their first medium. That's a fancy way of saying that people know Avril Lavigne as a teen star, so for a while she'll probably play roles like Heather that don't challenge the public image she already has.

It can be done. Mark Wahlberg is a great example of someone who's done it beautifully. Wahlberg was a teen star known as Marky Mark during the 1980s and early 1990s. His pop songs and dance moves made him an icon of the times. Had he tried to cross into movies then, he undoubtedly would have played punky teen roles that didn't challenge his pop-star image. Jump to a few years later, and people had all but forgotten his teen image. He's now successfully cast in a wide variety of roles. It may be that Avril Lavigne, like Mark Wahlberg, will need some time to grow and develop before she can make great changes to her public persona and expand the roles people will accept her playing.

On the other hand, if anyone can burst a mold and do exactly what they want to do, it's Avril Lavigne!

Chapter Four

What Can a Young Artist Learn from Avril Lavigne?

Maybe you're reading this book because you're more than just a fan—you're an aspiring performer. If so, good for you! One of the best things you can do for yourself is to learn everything you can about the music scene and the people who navigate it successfully. Reading this book, and this chapter in particular, demonstrates that you are open to and interested in learning more about the things that can make a musician successful.

Practice, Practice, Practice

Performers have a famous saying:

> **Q:** "Do you know the quickest way to Carnegie Hall?"
>
> **A:** "Practice, practice, practice."

Lavigne has a look of intense concentration as she rehearses at the World Music Awards.

Singers keep sharing this joke because it's so very true. If you plan on being a performer, you'll need to develop strong practice habits. Practice is important because it builds performance skills and confidence and teaches you the music you'll need to know when it comes time to perform. Avril Lavigne is a good example of how to do just that.

One of the first things we read about Lavigne in this book was that she started practicing at an early age. In chapter one, she talked about how she and her parents saw to it that she made time to practice and stayed dedicated to rehearsing her songs every day. In recent interviews, too, she talks about practicing and working hard.

Connect with the Right People

When asked by Lilly Cooper, a twelve-year-old interviewer, for her advice for young singers, Lavigne answered, as quoted in the London *Independent*, "Just be motivated, and just do as much as you can to get yourself heard and get your music heard. Hopefully you'll meet the right person at the right time and the right person will hear your music."

It's sure been true for her. Her career really got going when influential people began to hear her sing. And it's just as true for the rest of us. None of us can make it entirely on our own. We

need to connect with powerful people who see our talent, believe in us, and have our best interest at heart. In Lavigne's case, this happened repeatedly. First, there was a folk singer in her own community who started

Lavigne greets fans outside the MTV Studios in New York City.

introducing her around. Then, soon after, she was "discovered" by a manager while singing at a local bookstore. Then, that manager introduced her to higher-ups at Arista Records.

This isn't to say that young musicians should make friends with everyone who says they can help them be successful. Quite the contrary. It's important to discern which people are going to be the right people. They should really have decision-making power, strong personal connections, and your best interest at heart. Sometimes, in the heat of the moment, it's tough to decide if people meet all three qualifications. Whether or not you feel sure, it's a good idea to talk all decisions like this over with a few trusted adults. They should always know about other adults with whom you're developing a working relationship, and they'll help you make wise, safe decisions.

Appreciate Help When You Get It

When people help you reach your dreams, be sure to thank them for their help. There are lots of ways to express thanks. One is to say it with words, but there are other ways, and Avril Lavigne serves as an informative example here, too.

In this case, it's possible that Lavigne is more of an example of what not to do—specifically in terms of the people who may have helped her write some of her songs. If it's true that the folks at the Matrix were a significant help to her in writing some of her most popular songs, then it seems like the least she could do is willingly give these people credit and thanks for the part they played in helping her climb the charts. If she had, perhaps they'd still be helping her write hit songs, and she wouldn't be experiencing as much bad press.

Of course, we don't know what really happened in this case. But if it is true that she had help, she should certainly feel good about acknowledging it. It's the right thing to do, and it makes people want to help you become a star. Everyone likes recognition, even the people who help you attain it.

HINT

If you're new to the idea of practicing every day and if you're excited about Avril Lavigne as a role model, you might try this trick. Write the words "Avril practices" next to a picture of Avril Lavigne. Post it somewhere where you're likely to see it, and use it as an inspiring reminder of your new dedication to practice.

Lavigne shines with star quality in this photo taken at Z100's Jingle Ball in 2007.

Be Yourself

One thing about which there is no debate is Avril Lavigne's willingness to be herself. Her fans love her for it. Other singers take their clothes off to sell records, but not Lavigne. Other pop stars do drugs to have fun and fit in, but not Lavigne. She has standards and values that ring true for her, and she doesn't compromise them. People admire that. That has been a big part of what makes young fans—and their parents—appreciate her as a role model.

"Be yourself" would be another great thing to write next to a picture of Avril Lavigne. That way, every time you see it, you can be inspired not to be just like her, but to be just like you. The world's already got an Avril Lavigne, and she rocks. But we're all still waiting to see your star shine! How will you rock?

Timeline

August 2002 Lavigne wins an MTV Video Music Award for Best New Artist.

December 2002 Lavigne wins Best Female Performer and Best New Artist, *Rolling Stone* magazine.

April 2003 Lavigne wins four Juno awards.

September 2004 Lavigne wins Best Pop/Rock Artist at the World Music Awards.

April 2005 She wins Favorite Female Singer at the Kids' Choice Awards.

November 2007 She wins MTV Europe Music Awards for Most Addictive Track ("Girlfriend") and Solo Artist of the Year.

Discography

2002 *Let Go* (Arista Records)

2003 *My World* DVD (Arista Records)

2004 *Under My Skin* (Arista Records)

2007 *The Best Damn Thing* (Arista Records)

Glossary

anti-establishment Going against authority or mainstream culture.

artists and repertoire representative (A&R) An artist's manager. This person takes on the duty of furthering an artist's career.

aspiring Striving to reach a specific goal.

body of work A collection of all the things an artist produces. In the case of Avril Lavigne, this includes song lyrics, recordings, videos, DVDs, and film performances.

bubblegum pop Popular music that is highly produced and appeals to mostly young fans.

genre A style or category. Musical genres include rock and roll, country, punk, and jazz.

medium In art, a particular mode of artistic expression.

persona The personality an artist makes known to the public. While it may be very close to a performer's true personality, there is usually something a little bigger than life about the persona he or she shares with the public.

punk A musical genre popular since the 1970s, it usually features fast drums, loud guitar, and screaming vocals.

single A song released for play on the radio.

For More Information

Billboard
49 Music Square West
Nashville, TN 37203
(615) 321-4240
Web site: http://www.
   billboard.com
Organization that charts popular music of all genres.

Canadian Academy of
   Recording Arts and Sciences
345 Adelaide Street West
2nd Floor
Toronto, ON M5V 1R5
Canada
(416) 485-3135
Web site: http://www.
   junoawards.ca
Canadian organization for the
   study and recognition of
   excellence in recording.

MTV
1515 Broadway
New York, NY 10017
Web site: http://www.mtv.com
Cable channel featuring music
   and music-related program-
   ming. Pop culture authority
   and designator of the MTV
   Music Video Awards.

Web Sites

Due to the changing nature of
Internet links, Rosen Publishing
has developed an online list of
Web sites related to the subject
of this book. This site is
updated regularly. Please use
this link to access the list:

http://www.rosenlinks.com/
   cmtm/avla

For Further Reading

Bogdanov, Vladimir, Chris Woodstra, and Stephen Thomas Erlewine, eds. *All Music Guide to Rock: The Definitive Guide to Rock, Pop, and Soul*. San Francisco, CA: Backbeat Books. 2002.

Cross, Alan. *20th Century Rock and Roll—Alternative Rock*. Burlington, ON: Collector's Guide Publishing, Inc., 2000.

D'Errico, Camilla, and Joshua Dysart. *Avril Lavigne's Make 5 Wishes*. New York, NY: Manga Trade Paperback, 2007.

English, Tim. *Sounds Like Teen Spirit: Stolen Melodies, Ripped-Off Riffs, and the Secret History of Rock and Roll*. Lincoln, NE: iUniverse, 2007.

Massey, Howard. *Behind the Glass: Top Record Producers Tell How They Craft the Hits*. Milwaukee, WI: Backbeat Books, 2000.

Ramone, Phil. *Making Records*. New York, NY: Hyperion, 2007.

Tracy, Kathleen. *Avril Lavigne: A Blue Banner Biography*. Hockessin, DE: Mitchell Lane Publishers, 2004.

Whitburn, Joel. *Joel Whitburn Presents a Century of Pop Music: Year-by-Year Top 40 Rankings of the Songs & Artists That Shaped a Century*. Menomonee Falls, WI: Record Research, 1999.

Bibliography

"Avril Lavigne Marries Deryck Whibley." *People*, July 17, 2006. Retrieved January 25, 2008 (http://www.people.com/people/article/0,26334,1214386,00.html).

Blashill, Pat. "Album Review: *Let Go.*" *Rolling Stone*, July 2, 2002.

Cooper, Tim. "Oh Sister, What Art Thou?" *Independent* (London). Retrieved January 25, 2008 (http://www.independent.co.uk/arts-entertainment/music/features/avril-lavigne-o-sister-what-art-thou-527908.html).

Dougatz, Chad. "Avril Lavigne's Career Started in Hometown Church." Yahoo! Music, February 21, 2003. Retrieved January 25, 2008 (http://music.yahoo.com/read/news/12043171).

Erlich, Dimitri. "Avril Lavigne: Does This Pop Punkette Deserve a Grammy, or to Be Grounded?" *Interview*, March 2003 (http://www.ctv.ca/servlet/ArticleNews/story/CTVNews/20070704/Avril_Lavigne_070704/20070704?hub = Entertainment).

Halpern, Shirley. "Spotlight on . . . Avril Lavigne." *Entertainment Weekly*, April 13, 2007.

Robins, Dereck. "Avril's Twin Ambitions." *Sun* (London), May 23, 2006. Retrieved January 25, 2008 (http://www.thesun.co.uk/sol/homepage/showbiz/bizarre/online/article49155.ece).

Index

About the Author

Sarah Sawyer has a B.A. degree in vocal performance from Maryville College and years of vocal studio training. She is also an arts and lifestyle writer who has written for and about numerous bands and artists.

Photo Credits

Cover, p. 1 © Frank Micelotta/AMA/Getty Images for AMA; pp. 4–5, 9, 10, 17, 20, 41 © WireImage; p. 8 http://en.wikipedia.org/wiki/Image:Belleville_City_Hall.JPG; pp. 12, 24, 28, 37, 38 © Getty Images; p. 25 © Michael Ochs Archives/Getty Images; p. 32 © Kevin Mazur/WireImage; p. 33 © FilmMagic/Getty Images; p. 34 © DreamWorks. Courtesy Everett Collection.

Designer: Gene Mollica; **Editor:** Peter Herman